I am no
battlefield
but a
forest
of trees
growing

I am no battlefield but a forest of trees growing

Elvis Alves

10/21/21

Dear Naomi,
Thanks for being a member
of the chopin community.
Congrats on the recent achievements.
I wish you continued success.
Best,

Franciscan University Press

Franciscan University Press
1235 University Boulevard
Steubenville, OH 43952
740-283-3771

Distributed by:
The Catholic University of America Press
c/o HFS
P.O. Box 50370
Baltimore, MD 21211
800-537-5487

Library of Congress Cataloging-in-Publication Data
Names: Alves, Elvis, author.
Title: I am no battlefield but a forest of trees growing / by Elvis Alves.
Description: Steubenville, OH : Franciscan University Press ; Baltimore,
MD : Distributed by The Catholic University of America Press c/o HFS ,
[2018] | Series: Winner of the Jacopone da Todi Poetry Prize
Identifiers: LCCN 2018010341 | ISBN 0999513419 (978-0-9995134-1-5)
Subjects: LCSH: Faith—Poetry. | Responsibility—Poetry. | Change—
Poetry. | Spiritual life—Poetry.
Classification: LCC PS3601.L8795 A6 2018 | DDC 811/.6—dc23
LC record available at https://lccn.loc.gov/2018010341

Text and Cover Design: Kachergis Book Design

Cover Image: *Female Torso II*, 1928/1932, Kasimir Malevich.
Photo: akg-images.

Printed in the United States of America.

ISBN: 978-0-9995134-1-5

For my daughter, Maleeha

And may you in your innocence
sail through this to that.

—Lucille Clifton, "Blessing the Boats"

Contents

Acknowledgments

I am grateful to the editors of the following journals and magazines for supporting my work: *Transition, Sojourners, StepAway Magazine, Huizache, Four Chambers, The Caribbean Writer, Mom Egg Review, The Good Men Project,* and many more. *The New Southern Fugitives* published "Cowboy Neil @ Ground Zero," "King Tut," and "Gaze," also present in this volume.

Thank you, dear family and friends, for your love—it has carried me through this to that many times over: Dana Britton-Alves, Maleeha, Jaedan, Marcel Alves, Shelly Alves, Otis Alves, Wynita Alves, O'Ryan, Jacob, Malachi, Dereyanah, Ann Fraser, Sigman David, Desiree Liverpool, Audrey Fredericks Edwards, the Goodluck Family, the Britton Family, Winston Williams, Dolores Lindsay, Fidelis Ojevwe, Eugene "Bernie" Kendrick, and Dionne Dixon.

I am fortunate that the following writers are my friends: Cheryl Boyce-Taylor, Keisha-Gaye Anderson, Cynthia Manick, Jessica Goodfellow, Sam Moodie Vasquez, Annette Vendrys Leach, Tishon Woolcock, Bernadette McBride, Steve Nolan, Jacqueline Bishop, Charlie Bondhus, Helene Cardona, and Terry Culleton.

A special note of gratitude goes to the faculty, staff, and students of George School, an intentional community where transformative justice is the norm. You gave me wings as an educator, and for this I am grateful.

Thank you to Sarah Wear, David Craig, Ashleigh McKown, and others associated with Franciscan University Press for your help in putting this book into the world.

And to you, reader, thank you.

I am no
battlefield
but a
forest
of trees
growing

Aliens

They are all around.
I swear I see one every
now and then.

They blend in.
Some are kin
and wear the
same skin.

Where two or three
are gathered, aliens
are there too.

Parchman Prison

Nine miles from Tutwiler, Mississippi, 2017

Built to last, hold bodies as a hole that runs
to infinity and back. Black gold never sold.

Time was never enough until time stops in here and you
are surrounded by selves without direction to go beyond

a state of degeneration. Authorized penetration of body, mind,
and soul. Nothing has ever been good to the person

behind your doors. Nothing comes out alive. A refuse that society
does not want back. A thing unlike other things. The bottom of a

swamp built beneath a swamp. You get what you want
except for freedom because it comes with a price. Your body, mind,

and soul. All that is glued together, the mind breaks from. All that the
mind breaks from is glued together. We stick together like glue. We fight

for breath. A taste of air. A taste of anything that does not remind us
of the years a judge wrote on paper, sealed our destiny, and shut us up here.

A Killing in Clarksdale

Clarksdale, Mississippi, 2017

A black carpenter shot and killed
a black lawyer. The lawyer owed
him money for building his mansion.

Ben said that he does not know what
he would have done if he were in the
same situation as the carpenter. Ben
is a carpenter.

Ms. Houston, the electrician, said
that the lawyer built his house where
the white folks lived and screwed
over many people in Clarksdale.

Nat said the lawyer, once shot, escaped
to his office and retrieved a gun from
his desk and fired at the carpenter.
He missed.

The incident happened at a deposition
hearing. The judge told the lawyer he
had 5 years to pay the carpenter. The
lawyer said that he would pay
the carpenter a lump sum on the last
day of the 5 years.

Nat said that at the end of the hearing, the
carpenter exited the room with his lawyer,
who is also the mayor of Clarksdale and a
friend of Morgan Freeman (They co-own
Ground Zero). But the carpenter said he
forgot something in the room. He returned
to claim the life of the black lawyer.

Cowboy Neil @ Ground Zero

Clarksdale, Mississippi, 2017

Cowboy Neil asks his guitar Louise
what it wants him to do to it before
playing it with his tongue. The white
students got a kick out of this and
couldn't stop talking about it. One
wrote in his journal that Cowboy Neil
went down on his guitar and that he
had met God @ Ground Zero. In the
white mind, the black body is a god
and is hated.

Stop Start

Rhythm in heart.
        Pull up, come again.
This time, begin anew
        stop & start.
Bring something back
        from the grave.
Kick life into it.
        Make it swell
w/ joy
        and yell,
"*I am here, again.*"

Who Will Survive ...

McDonald's
Guns
Drugs
War
~~Peace~~
Injustice
Police
Annihilation
Prison
Dementia
Integration
Colonization
Globalization
Nepotism
Schools
Government
Capitalism
Alzheimer
Pharmaceutical Companies
Bad News
Discrimination
The Crab Barrel
Betrayal
Hennessy
Crack
Churches
You
Me
Us
?

System of Symmetry

Binding thoughts together like stars dancing
in synchrony, the cosmos reminds us that we

are not alone when we are alone.

I will forget everything about this day, because
to live is to forget.

If memories are the only things worth holding on to,
you are here though you sleep among strangers.

Tell me you won't fall from the system of symmetry.
If you do, I will catch you.

Learning to Play Poker on a Native American Reservation

Kayenta, Arizona, 2015

Call my bluff, my poker face is not rigid.
I need to not smile or laugh when my hand
is good, when my hand is bad.

I keep looking for pairs but the high card
is what appears.

I trade for more than what I can afford.
The other players ante up.

They know me, I fold.

I am learning to play poker on a Native American reservation
where playing cards are kept from the hand's

reach, along with cough medicine and certain types
of cleaning products in grocery stores.

Poker is a game of chance, like life is a game of chance,
especially on a reservation or anywhere else where there is
poverty.

I am told that drugs move through here.

I see obese people and don't question why they are obese,
just like I don't question the tidbit of information about
drug trafficking.

I, too, am passing through, learning to play poker and looking
at the people as they look at me.

King Tut

Tutwiler, Mississippi, 2017

She wants to bring a dog back to Philadelphia with her.
She calls it King Tut, short for Tutwiler, after finding
it on the streets, or so she claims. I interject, "do you

know if he has a home?" She couldn't answer. The
thought has yet to appear in her head (until I give
birth to it). I think of Europeans arriving on the shores

of Africa to confiscate black bodies, asking nothing of
their culture, history, or not wanting to be owned.

Kwame

The school suspended Kwame.
Kicked his black ass to the curb.

Book bag. Saxophone.
He cried in the car.

I watch him disappear into
the night's cold air at the train station,
going to his mama in Philadelphia.

Invention of Mathematics

They stop to move again, to reach wider shores
like the wings of a bird.

They are the invention of mathematics.
They know the color of the dirt of Abyssinia. It is
their skin. And kin.

Say no more. What is felt cannot be written.
All is lost in translation but not in the transporting of souls,
of names, of history in the dark caverns of empire-building

vessels that sailed from there to here, beyond the knowing.

Walk and Don't Look Back

Peter Tosh tells Mick Jagger. Don't look back like
the nameless woman who turned to salt which is
a good thing because salt is the spice of life
and in turning into a clump of salt she became more
than Lot's wife. Taste salt and live. It is the earth. The
earth is salt and so are humans. That's why we taste
each other to feel alive.

Desultory Moment of Cognition

Shackled below waves that clash against the chambers
of my heart, I drown in despair not knowing it would come
to this, a desultory moment of cognition. The diagnosis. No cure.
Just progress in the parochial use of the term and at the end of
which is death. A noose on the neck. Explosion of a chemical-filled
bomb. Sorrow overload. There is more. Remember, this does not
stop nor does it get better with time (like wine or age—maybe just
wine). It becomes more of itself. It eats at the world as the world eats
the mind until death and life mean clarity. To live is to die.
To die is to live. We name that which we know to make sense
of what we do not know. Then there is this. A thing that calls from
the beyond with a voice familiar to he who sleeps with noise and silence.
A fancy title. Something scribbled above this poem. But still something,
if for a moment.

I Done Got Over

"Johnny, be good," my mother said to I when I left
for the shitty. I would become Johnny B. Goode, leader
of a reggae band. Playing the guitar and pedaling
ganja is all that I know. I met the blackheart man at a gig.
He introduced I to the teachings of Selassie I. I threw away the comb,
started to eat ital, and reasoned with a dawta I used to rub-a-dub with at
the club. She became I queen and I became her king. Soon we
have one big family. No money coming-in in this shitstem so I pedal
ganja and sing. Ba-be-wrong soldiers never liked I. They did not
want I dread & alive. They charged I for ganja and bring I in front of
a judge who had no empathy for I. Now I sit and serve I
sentence and think of I family and hope that the blackheart man
will come save I.

Run Go Tell

Blackheart man brings people to my door.
I give them the herb that they light with
fire that engulfs the entire shitty.

A holy conflagration is what the newspapers
call the happening.

I am now in a room I cannot break from.
The guards bring food colored with spit.

I cannot die and rise like Jesus. I am a Rastaman.
I live for i-ver.

The blackheart man will come, I know. He was
here yesterday. One of the guards told me this
even though he was not supposed to. The truth
cannot hide for i-ver.

Feet are coming toward me. They bring some kind
of news. I am to be hung tomorrow. This is what
they will say to me, a branded hot-stepper.

Run Come See

"Guess you gonna die before the dollar," one of the guards
says as they lead I to the gallows. "You fren, the blackheart
man, he deh ah asylum," another chimed in.

They fed I pink blue yellow green soda and frankfurter the
night before. And called I choke-brain, even though I don't take
cocaine.

Nuff people run come see like when they run come see Selassie
at airport.

I mother beg the jailors to set I free. They give I twenty lashes, brand
hot-stepper 'pon I chest, and let I go.

I escaped to the hills to become a mystic man, sharp as a razor, ready to
cut them down.

Merchant Women of Ghana

Cape Coast, Ghana, 2016

Ladies with fruit stands on head stop me to
speak the few English that they know. They
are better than me.

They know some of my language. I know none
of theirs.

"She love you," one says, pointing to another who
hides behind a smile.

"She love you" becomes a passport to a land far from
here.

It is a familiar set of words my lover says to me at home,
far from here (replacing the she with I).

I wonder how she would react to the hearing of it from
the lips of another woman, directed at me.

I too am shy and so I hide behind an awkward smile,
wanting to leave but basking in the newfound role of

celebrity, surrounded by merchant women on the streets of
Cape Coast, who are willing to sell me their love

if I am willing to pay the price.

Stars

She is afraid of the future.
It is without name.
Yet to born.
I tell her that everything
comes from somewhere.
"A bang," she says
and I watch stars explode
in her eyes.

Dana

We are on this blue train.
You are my Naima. Pretty
as Queen Nefertiti. The prophet
had Khadijah and Aisha.
You are my Mona Lisa.
The sun in my day.
Your love I desire. For it
I pray. The gods brought
you to me. I receive the gift
that you are with gratitude
and cheers and promise to
shower you with love and
nothing less.

A Fly in a Room of Flies

She says I am w/o conscience and my name
is written in hell. I do not believe her because

hell is here on earth and I am smiling as I walk
through it.

She gives me hell but I do not say this, at least not
now. I am tired of fighting and of being fought.

I do not know what will come from my mouth. I
bite my tongue. It bleeds the truth.

We fight to make love, embrace each other in the
power the world wants to take from us because
our skin is black, the color of gods.

I tell myself that she is worth holding on to. We
are all that we have. Why do we fight?

I call my mother and talk to her but she
does not know what I am saying. I call because
she is the only woman that listens to me.

I walk away from my problems but
they follow me. They do not know how to give up
the chase and so I give in to them. They become

who I am and I become who they are. How does
it feel to be a problem?

You are the problem, she says to me. We are tearing
each other down to build each other up.

The world is cold and your kindness is the blanket
I want to wrap myself in. I tell her this in bed.

She rises. Looks me in the eyes. Lies down and goes
to sleep. I stay awake, look at the ceiling and wonder
how it feels to be a fly in a room of flies.

Chinese Acrobat

She stands and watches the years crumble behind her.
How many ladders she has climbed. Flips made. Hoops
jumped through. Twirls. Kicks. Balancing this and that.

But never life. Always on the go. Collect money for the
boss. He who owns her. Then he no longer needs her.
Her replacement. Younger. Willing to do all that she

she can do and more. The acrobat exits with grace. Bows
one last time to the crowd she always pleases. Was trained
to please. And enters a world she never had time to learn.

She stands years later. Wonders how she survived
between then and now. Gracefully, she thinks and
holds her breath. And exhales.

An Incident in the Mail Room

Jim told Henry not to watch porn at work.
I wondered why he took so long to admonish
Henry.

Perhaps he was busy ordering me around to
lift and distribute boxes of mail that arrived
daily.

I worked in the mail room for work study. A title
that says poor students must do work for scholarships
that the school gives them.

I would look in the direction of Jim and Henry's office
and see naked white women on Henry's computer screen.

Professors would come into the mail room and talk to
Jim and Henry. Did they see the nude women? Did they care?

They got their mail from me. They hardly said anything to
me. I provided a service. Students too got their mail from me.

They talked to me but did not say much. I worked with Suzette,
a blond girl from California, who, one day, laughed hysterically

while she and I discussed *David Walker's Appeal*. I asked her what
was funny about the black struggle. She couldn't answer my question.

Soon after this incident, I talked to Jim, he was the supervisor, not about
Henry's continued watching of porn in the mail room but about Suzette.

I told him that he needs to level the workload in giving Suzette equal
work as me, that she too can lift boxes and distribute mail as often
as he tells me to do these things.

He did not say anything. He shook his head like Henry had shook his
head when he told him to stop watching porn in the mail room.

Kingdom Protista

Kingdom Protista is known to the people against
the walls of humanity fighting for survival.

Don't smile. It weighs you down. Tells others more
about you than you want known, like a proud mother
bearing her soul.

Darkness is in everything. Life is carried beyond the horizon of
thoughts.

In Kingdom Protista, hands grow weary with the days,
and pray for relief.

Tomorrow the sun will rise and you will witness it without trying.

Professor M_____

It was in my second year of college when we met in the corridor
of the lecture hall. It was a hot spring day. I remember. I also
remember you telling me of the gifted student who once studied
philosophy with you and who was gunned down on the streets near
Columbia University. You said that he was robbed, and walked away,
but decided to throw the few dollar notes still in his pocket at the robber.
Offended, the gunman took his life with a single bullet. His promising life.
Was he black? Yes, the perpetrator was black, you corrected me. And I
apologized then, not for the mistake but for the black body that I am. In
that instant I read your mind that I was linked with the perpetrator. Why
else tell me the story? I could not be the promising student even though I
was now studying philosophy with you and you once remarked in class
that you turned to me to move the class along when you felt it was stuck. I felt
proud. I felt used. At the hearing of this. But it is the interaction with you
in the corridor of the lecture hall that stayed with me throughout the years.
I want to tell you that between then and now, I have reeducated myself and
have tasted freedom in embracing my blackness, unapologetically.

Gaze

Clarksdale, Mississippi, 2017

How does it feel to see
me a novelty?
A strange man walking
through your world.
Your gaze vaporous.
Empty of power.
Full of envy.
My crown of hair
dark and beautiful
as my skin.
I am walking.
I am leaving marks.
A tornado passing through.
The weatherman failed to
warn you in advance.
You are surprised.
Confounded by the sight
of this black body.

Slapboxing with Jesus

Why not?
That is what we do in the hood,
show and spread love with every hit.

Slapboxing toughens Jesus. He's a
wimpy kid. What else to expect from
a guy without a male role model at home?

Papi said that Joseph died at Bellevue. Marta,
the nosy neighbor, said that Mary kicked
him to the curb because he couldn't help
with rent.

A person's status depends on salary and Joseph
had no dough.

Whatever happened to him, he's gone.
Ghost.

Jesus needs saving. Slapboxing will knock
sense into him.

The Lower Body Meridian

After A Tribe Called Quest's The Low End Theory

Clouds are there.
They flutter when touched.

What words spell relief?

I tend not to believe everything.
But some things are worth holding on to.

There is intrinsic value in experience.
Life can appeal in several measures.

Intuition is reminder that I know before told.

The clouds are appearing and disappearing.
They write your name. Is this the same as relief?

My lips confess what the heart knows.
Love is found in the lower body meridian.

IoT

No submission
necessary with the
feature you want to
change, hone.
This is the Internet of
things, a language not
spoken, not felt but
we are told is
everything.

Return of the Prodigal Son

I have buried you in the land of the forgiven,
a place where you are responsible for your
resurrection.

I have turned to live what is left of this life
with peace and harmony with self and others

that seek my upliftment as much as I seek their
upliftment.

A return of the prodigal son from the unknown. I am a
journey that has many beginnings, no battlefield
but a forest of trees growing.

Gospel of Truth

They come to us
seeking life because
they are dead. Beware
of the bullshit they
bring for they believe
that we are the ones
in need of saving.

Jungle Groove

After James Brown

A sermon that tells you
get in the water. Be

a sex machine. This
groove that the godfather
of soul captures is no

panacea but springs
funk and spreads energy

deep enough not to be
uprooted by the ploys

of the man and his system.
Get in the water, he yells

from the street corner where
the band gathers. The funky

drummer is on something
funky. This is the spell the

church fears. Music that is the
savior of the people in the jungle

they did not create but must survive.

Astral

The years spent kneading what you know into commerce
with hope for reward only to realize true investment is not

possible because you are working to make a living. How
should living work? We should learn to tear the sky apart

and become like the stars. Astral. Vast as that which is unknown
even though it begs to be known. A god among gods. Or, the

good that is sufficient because it is good, leaving Plato or some
other mind aghast and humble.

For the Red Hot Chili Peppers

Whose pain did you borrow?
Or, is it your own?

Your tongues lick the salt of
earth, cut grass, and a wall of

fire burns everything down.
This pain you found under a bridge.

Needle pricks skin and sinks in,
then a rush to the beyond.

And you are pulled back
to this life. Augmented pain.

Nothing changed. You are alive
for now.

Jessie Mae Hemphill

Country woman with steel
in throat that reverberates

with notes. She-wolf.
Soul city shaker. Shake
down party. Deep South

blues. Rebel woman.
Bad mama jama.

Canyon Lady

After Joe Henderson

The world weighs the same
as a feather when you are in flight.

What stands you still and pushes you
around the sun w/o order?

Beneath the asking is a vacuum
waiting for nothing to fill it,

as ants march to their death in
in single file.

What face you bring when the hands
of time say it is time beyond time;

Take your seat,
take off.

Your wings are heavy and strong,
have staying power, a canyon.

Scratch

For Lee "Scratch" Perry, the Upsetter

I come to make Babylon bend him
knees and worship Selassie I.

Free up the herb and I will promote it.
Smoke it.

Babylon is a vampire, sucking the
blood of the sufferahs.

I am the upsetter, ready to conquer
this captive land w/ word, sound, &
power.

M2M

Can they make love? Will they replace humans?
Automatons w/o heart cannot breed but multiply,

populate a city with infrastructures that keep selves
safe, tell when repair is needed. The future is here with

outstretched hands. It is too late to turn back, the past
cannot be recaptured but improved upon.

Twilight Zone

For Wynita

Far into the twilight zone
a hole beams evidence
that they are there, people
who never left.

Do you believe?

To question is to doubt.
Don't ask but seek the
knowing.

Nightlife

With minds lost to liquid no longer
in cups but in our stomachs,

we dance the night away with
a high. I touch her lips with my
tongue and she begs me to dig deeper.

I am looking for love,
a nugget of wisdom,
or something else valuable.

I crave silence.
To suspend everything
and live in the moment.

Third Eye

We watch the sun watch us
then disappear beyond the
horizon.

There are faces in
the moon.

Trees dance whether
we are looking or not.

The ocean is a drum that
speaks a sacred language.

Listen. You'd hear nature at
her best.

See with eyes and mind.

The third eye is big and
beautiful and lives in you.

Technology (IoT)

Spell the instance
below an ocean of wants.

Tie the truth and throw it
overboard.

It will sink in the heart of history
to rise again like cries of ancestors
from the depth of where they are.

Things hidden grow wings,
sprout from the ground.

I tell you this because I cannot
tell you otherwise.

Knowing is not technology.
Wisdom is gold.

Mirrors

When you believe everything
you are near the unborn.

Innocence is a project.
Something to work on
to make real.

Much happens
since birth to keep it
out of reach.

This is conforming, not
wanting to stand alone
because we know otherwise;

all animals move in droves.
Survival instinct.

Escape is in books
& fantasies. But life has a
way of pulling us back

and setting mirrors so
we can see.

James Baldwin Meets w/ Elijah Muhammad and They Talk Black Power

EM: The black man needs to regain his
prominence in the world. Slavery, colonization,
ghettoization stunted his growth. The
teachings of Islam are here to correct this.

JB: I am not interested in religion. My concerns
lie in the plan that would allow us as a people,
as black people, to move forward in this land. I
know what the Christian church has done to my
people, and I am afraid that Islam, or your Nation
of Islam, might do worse if black folks start following
it in droves.

EM: Speak of what you know. You know the Christian
faith but not Islam. This is the original religion of the
original people. The Nation of Islam put forth economic
upliftment by way of race upliftment.

JB: Your plan is one of separation. The black man cannot
move forward without the white man, and the white man
cannot move forward without the black man. We are bound
in brotherhood, both white and black.

EM: Move forward? These words are not in the white man's
vocabulary unless they relate to himself and to his people. He
has left the black man behind.

JB: I do not think we are on board with the same program.

EM: Yes we are, my brother. We are talking about
black power.

White Spaces / Black Bodies

White spaces were not made for
black bodies. Should we impose,
or create our own? If I knew
you were coming I would have
baked you a cake. Get on board
the status quo. Don't sit at the
table, the food is not seasoned.
Enough. And you are not welcome.

Jubilation

Joy flows from within to
the outside world. Has the
potential to infect everyone.

God wears the face of a
smiling child.

The earth replenishes
itself. No need to save it.

All you need to do is take in
what is to take in.

You say nothing has meaning.
Perhaps everything has meaning

and you find the answer or reason
when you stop looking.

Ephemeral

I pay the man at the counter
for the purchase.

A normal exchange.

I owe him something for the
things in the basket in my hands.

I leave and make do with what I
have until I have them no more.

Everything is ephemeral.

This is what I tell myself about life
and its happenings.

A lesson worth knowing.

Prayer

Tear us not apart
at the seams of
injustice but
make us strong
and courageous
like ancestors who
fought because their
lives and our lives
depended on it.

Easter

I wake to a song in the next room.
Time to celebrate resurrection.

That good triumphs evil
and there's hope for a safe world.

Empathy, I tell my students, must
be a must.

They are familiar with reducing humans
to numbers and formulas.

Money, for them, is power.

I tell them that life is a gift
worth cherishing above all else.

Oven

I feel for you. I think I love you.

——CHAKA KHAN

You called and said you think the oven was
left on. You were at your sister's place miles
away, in the backwoods of Upstate New York.

Your grandmother said that you should stay.
That you are with child and to take the train
back to New York City would be too much stress
on you, on the growing fetus.

You said later that I volunteered to drive three states
to touch a cold oven but I did not argue, even though
I do not remember volunteering.

I do remember driving and touching a
cold oven to return to my car and drive back to
Pennsylvania (I had to teach the next day).

It was under a 10-minute stay in New York City.
The shortest. Ever.

I feel for you. I think I love you.

Sacrifice

The women undressed before entering the water.
Those on the shore prayed for safety, theirs and that of
the women in the water.

A day will come when no one would remember the
sacrifice and what came from it.

There are still questions even though everything falls into place
eventually, a hand holding a hand holding another hand.

The witnesses prayed and sang until the dawn drew them home
to sleeping children and husbands awaiting news of the sacrifice.

But they did not say anything, and the men left for the fields where
their sweat become one with earth.

At noon, a girl was found crying under a tree. She had seen
something move across the land with the clouds and had begged to go.
Her tears are lost memory. She was unable to say more.

Soon, all animals ran east and a wind picked up that did not stop
blowing, and the women who entered the water reappeared
clothed with the sun before everything went dark for a moment that

seemed like eternity interrupted by lightning, announcing new knowledge.

Sainthood of Tupac

Police got all
eyez on me.

Want to stop
and frisk me in
this country built
on the backs of
people that look
like me.

When will this misery
stop? I'm calling for
truce but no one listens
to me.

They want to shoot
or put me away in
the penitentiary.
That's how they make
money for people that
look like them.

The rich start war.
The poor fight it.
Ain't that a bitch?

When will you see that
we are in the same boat?
I can never kill a brother if
he is close to me.

Is this fantasy? Reality calls
me to the streets with a gun
on my waist.

I ain't no saint so I am not leaving
earth without bringing some of
my enemies with me.

There is a war in the streets
so that the police can bother me
but there's none on poverty.

Someone help me understand
this mystery.

I ain't no saint.
There can't be peace
without equal rights
and justice.

Holler if you hear me.
It is time we take
what was never given us.

From slave ships,
back of buses, chokeholds,
and handcuffs, this shit
must stop.

I ain't no saint. Only
God can judge me.
Holler if you hear me.

What the Future Says

Lines on palms say what is to come and where we have been.
Nothing is new under the sun. Life is a circle unbroken.

We create mantras that remind us of what we want out of
Life. Or, what life wants out of us.

Even when it is possible to forget, we cling to memories that say
who we are and will be.

Worship

We pray to gain strength.
Talk with lips bitten by
the wind. Worship to
celebrate life and its
mysteries.

Come down from
your high chair. The
sky will rend your
heart.

Hair on our heads
belie a familiar story.
We grow into many
tomorrows.

Sing and dance beyond
space and time. Gather
in the now that which
came before and will
come.

We are strong. Enough
to withstand the storm.

Burning Spear

Music is a spear that digs
deep in the soil of the soul.

When something grows,
it pulls from a source.

What is your source?
What keeps you afloat
when life has you down?

Reggae has power. And soul.
Who is afraid of it? The government
not for the people.

Music is seed planted
before the forest appears.

It moves my soul.
The spear that keeps
burning.

Resist

The notion that you can belong to someone else
and not yourself has not vacated the mind of he
who thinks himself above everyone.

The master class. These are people not planted
on firm ground. They prop themselves on the
backs and lives of others. Of the lower class.

But they need cutting down to size. Seized
with fear, they create a buffer zone.

Give a poor man a badge and a gun. Call him
officer. Same as overseer. Protector. Not of
common people. But of the wealth of the rich.

It is a crazy world. Right is wrong and wrong is
right. Who will fix it, sacrifice self for what is
perishing?

The question deserves an answer.
Something that says there is more to come.
Like the next life, siblings, or sound of gun reminding

people of the pledge to resist and survive
Armageddon & apocalypse.

Gifted Child

I am the son of
fathers past. Of
mothers carrying
the earth's energy,
pushing forward
ever. The promise
borne of sorrow
and toil. The coming
of wants never spoken.
He who belongs to
this and many moments.
A gifted child.
Prayed for. The end
before it begins. I
have always been.
Teach me truth.
Tell me that I am
greater than what
they tell me I am.
Open my hands.
Read my mind.
Push me toward
my destiny. Plant
wisdom in my life.
Water it so it
multiplies. Let
me not sink
but grow with
grace. Be a
provider of
what is needed
in my life
in this life
in these days
forever.

Immigrants

They come to this land to plant seeds
among weeds of racism trying to keep
them down.

They do not give in or up to the
pressure of the system of the man
wearing the cloak of injustice and
greed.

They suffer shame. Their spirits
get low but never low enough to
not rise again.

Children grow on their backs.
Their shoulders span generations.

They are fighters fighting to be free.
They hold a legacy hungry for

the fulfillment of promises made
to self before coming to these
shores.

The hope of tomorrows is on
their heads and seen in the eyes
of progeny.

They are one with their dreams,
forever rising.

Black boy in love

escapes to Central Park to be with
girl that has his heart.

His mother nags him to do chores,
wash dishes, clean up after himself

but what she really wants is for him
to be safe.

When he leaves for the park, she wonders
who will be afraid of his innocence and
rob it from him?

She tells him be careful. He says I am.

He goes into the woods surrounded by
a concrete jungle to emerge with a smile.

Did you kiss her? His mother asks.
She kissed me on the cheeks, he says.

Notes

"Aliens" borrows from the song "Aquemini," from the same-titled album by the rap group Outkast. Lines from the song go, "Alien can blend right in with your kin. Look again, 'cause I swear I see one every now and then."

"Stop Start" shares its title with a song by the Jazz musician Lee Morgan.

"Walk and Don't Look Back" is a title of a song and also a collaboration between Peter Tosh and the Rolling Stones.

"I Done Got Over," "Run Go Tell," and "Run Come See" serve as odes to the late, great reggae artist Peter Tosh. These poems contain album titles and lyrics from Tosh's songs, including "Johnny B. Goode," "Dread & Alive," "The Day the Dollar Dies," "Stepping Razor," "Pink blue yellow green soda and frankfurter," and "Mystic Man." The poems also reference *Blackheart Man*, a reggae album and song by Tosh's bandmate Bunny Wailer. "Hot Stepper" is a song by the reggae artist Gregory Isaacs on his *Night Nurse* album.

"Dana" references John Coltrane's album *Blue Train*. The song "Naima" was named after and dedicated to his wife. Dana is my wife's name.

In "A Fly in a Room of Flies," the verse "The world is cold and your love is a blanket I want to wrap myself in" was inspired by the song "The Abstract" by A Tribe Called Quest on their album *The Low End Theory*. The song states, "The world is kinda cold and the rhythm is my blanket."

"Slapboxing with Jesus" is named after the short story collection by Victor Levalle. It was first coined by the rapper Ghostface Killah in "Daytona 500," a song on his *Ironman* album: "I slapbox with Jesus, lick shots at Joseph." The verse "a person's status depends on salary" is taken from the song "Life's a Bitch" on the *Illmatic* album by Nas.

"James Baldwin Meets w/ Elijah Muhammad and They Talk Black Power" recollects the chapter in Baldwin's *Fire Next Time* where he met and was courted by Elijah Muhammad, then the leader of the movement, to join the Nation of Islam. Although Baldwin agreed with some of the standpoints of the Nation, he rejected membership, seeing it as too separatist.

"Black boy in love" is a protest poem, as are others in the collection, against the senseless killing of black and brown bodies.

About the Author

Elvis Alves was born in Guyana and raised in Brooklyn, New York. He is a graduate of Colgate University and Princeton Theological Seminary. Elvis is the author of the poetry collection *Bitter Melon* (Mahaicony Books, 2013) and the chapbook *Ota Benga* (Mahaicony Books, 2017). His poetry has appeared in several journals and magazines. Elvis lives in New York City with his family.